Mitsumasa Anno
ANNO'S COUNTING BOOK

Thomas Y. Crowell Company | New York

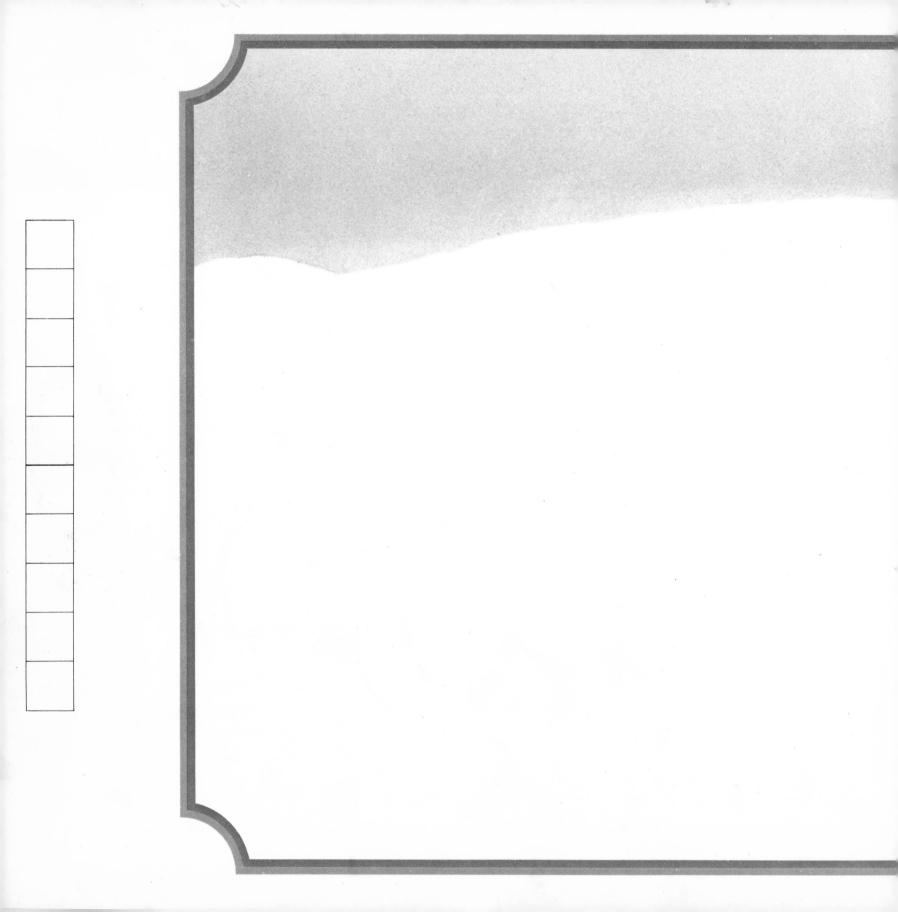

1

2

3

4

5

6

7

8

9

10

11

12

About Numbers

The pictures in this book show some of the things and events in nature and in their daily lives that may have led people to start counting with numbers. All this is usually taken for granted by adults, but it is useful for children just becoming acquainted with numbers to begin at the beginning, with the way that people first learned to count.

What are numbers? 1, 2, 3—these are only figures. One, two, three—these are only words. To learn what numbers really are, let's first imagine people back in the Stone Age, when they had to hunt and catch animals for their food. If people hunted deer, they could keep a record of how many deer they had caught by saving up the antlers. But antlers are hard to handle; small pebbles are much easier. Perhaps Stone Age people began to keep their records with pebbles rather like this:

What day:	How many deer caught:
o (First day)	o o o
o o (Second day)	
o o o (Third day)	o o o o o o
o o o o (Fourth day)	o o

To use one pebble to stand for one deer is called "one-to-one correspondence." And, of course, pebbles could be used to stand not only for deer but also for periods of time (days), for birds or men or even for such things as amounts of water. The above chart shows what is called "tallying" and it is this which enables the one-to-one correspondences to be made.

Then perhaps people began to compare how many pebbles there were in the different groups, so that they could tell, for example, that they had caught more deer yesterday than today. By using such one-to-one correspondences, by matching and comparing, they could count and add and subtract—all without using any words to stand for the numbers.

But eventually people realized that it would be more convenient to give special names to different-sized groups of pebbles, and to replace the pebbles themselves with words. Now they could express the same message in words instead of pebbles, like this:

What day:	How many deer caught:
First day	three
Second day	none
Third day	six
Fourth day	two

It was even more convenient when they began to replace the words with simple figures:

What day:	How many deer caught:
1	3
2	0
3	6
4	2

Of course, it is practically impossible to give a completely different name to each one of the infinity of possible numbers. The philosophers of ancient India discovered the wonderful concept of "zero." Then they found that if they combined "zero", or "0", with 1, 2, 3, 4, 5, 6, 7, 8, or 9, they could express just about any number they wanted to, quite simply. In the figure "10" the "0" really means a group of ten and no more. To express "10 and 1 more," or 11, the "0" is replaced by "1". To express "10 and 2 more," or 12, the "0" is replaced by "2". The number 57 means "five groups of ten and seven more." This was the birth of the decimal system. It allows us to express numbers of almost any size in a very simple way, by using just these nine digits plus zero in various combinations. Eventually hours, days, months, and years came to be numbered too.

M.A.